SCENES
*of America*

# TURN-OF-THE-CENTURY
# PHILADELPHIA

2358— *Fairmount Park, PHILA. PA.*

SCENES

*of America*

# TURN-OF-THE-CENTURY PHILADELPHIA

LYNN M. HOMAN AND THOMAS REILLY

Published by Arcadia Publishing
Charleston SC, Chicago IL, Portsmouth NH, San Francisco CA

Library of Congress control number: 2006926058

For all general information contact Arcadia Publishing at:
Telephone 843-853-2070
Fax 843-853-0044
E-mail sales@arcadiapublishing.com
For customer service and orders:
Toll-Free 1-888-313-2665

Visit us on the Internet at www.arcadiapublishing.com

*On the cover*: While other portions were not as commercially developed, this six-mile section of the Schuylkill River in Philadelphia was lined with factories, docks, and wharves.

# CONTENTS

# INTRODUCTION

By the end of the first quarter of the 20th century, Philadelphia had grown from a population of 4,000 in 1699 to approximately 2.5 million residents in the city and surrounding suburbs. Since its founding in 1683 by William Penn, an English Quaker, as the capital of his colony of Pennsylvania, the city had also drawn millions of visitors. The largest city in Pennsylvania, the third largest in America, and the eighth largest in the world, Philadelphia was a city with a rich history. A colony founded on religious freedom, Pennsylvania drew not just those of the Quaker faith but members of all religious denominations. The number and variety of churches in Philadelphia illustrated that diversity. At the start of the American Revolution, delegates from each of the colonies came to Philadelphia to participate in the Continental Congress. Following the war with England, Philadelphia became the first capital of the new nation. As the nation's center of government, the city drew even more visitors. Immigrants from throughout the world made Philadelphia their destination as well. As evidenced by Philadelphia's growth, many of those visitors returned to settle permanently.

Visitors to Philadelphia, whether tourists or businessmen, during the first quarter of the 20th century found a city undergoing great changes. Alterations occurred in almost every aspect of life. Many of the new residents were poor and unskilled, as compared to the earlier immigrants who brought with them expertise in various trades. New technologies altered modes of transportation; at the same time, traffic congestion increased. The city's skyline changed as new buildings soared to unprecedented heights. Boardinghouses still existed, but an increasing number of large hotels filled the center city. The cultural life of the city took on a new sophistication. Although still small town in nature in some ways, the City of Brotherly Love was rapidly taking on the appearance of a metropolis.

While the changes in the growing city had the greatest impact on the residents, visitors to Philadelphia were less affected. They saw only a diverse community filled with big-city amenities and small-town warmth, metropolitan attractions, and plenty of excitement. Then, as now, visitors remembered their trip through postcards and photographs of the places they had been, the sights they had seen, and the things they had done. For the visitor of today, many of those places and images no longer exist, victims of demolition, urban renewal, and a changing society. Yet through these postcards, carefully saved over the years, those visits to Philadelphia during the first quarter of the 20th century can be shared.

ONE

# TOURIST DESTINATIONS

Philadelphia's rich history drew many visitors with an interest in America's beginnings. Those with a love of military history could view the remaining buildings, sally ports, and gun emplacements of old Fort Mifflin. The fort was constructed during the 1770s on Mud Island, along the west bank of the Delaware River, to thwart British control of the Delaware and Schuylkill Rivers and prevent the capture of Philadelphia. The defensive strategy proved successful for a time, delaying the British until September 26, 1777, when they occupied the city. Fort Mifflin was finally captured in November, after which George Washington's troops retreated to Valley Forge. Badly damaged during the Revolutionary War, Fort Mifflin was rebuilt in 1798. Additional buildings, including an arsenal, storehouse, mess house, and magazines, were added during the 1800s.

Old Fort Mifflin, Philadelphia, Pa.

2383

The most popular of all Philadelphia destinations for visitors was, of course, Independence Hall. Originally built as the Pennsylvania State House, the brick building symbolized the American fight for freedom from British rule in the minds of many people. This postcard, the first in a series devoted to the subject, described Independence Hall as "the Birthplace of Liberty" and termed it the most famous building in America. Jointly designed by Andrew Hamilton, speaker of the State Assembly, and Edmund Woolley, the master builder who supervised its construction, the first phase began in 1732 and was completed in 1748. Between 1750 and 1753, the tower and steeple were added. Congress Hall, the adjoining building to the right, was built in 1789 and served as the meeting place of the United States Congress until the nation's capital relocated to Washington, D.C., in 1800. Old city hall (left) was completed in 1791 as the home of the United States Supreme Court. Scheduled for demolition and subdivision into building lots in 1816, the buildings and the square were purchased by the city in 1816 for $70,000.

Every bit as famous as Independence Hall was the Liberty Bell. Cast in England at the Whitechapel Foundry, the bronze bell cracked upon its first ringing in Philadelphia and was recast by John Pass and John Stow in 1753. Weighing more than 2,000 pounds, the bell was inscribed, "Proclaim liberty throughout all the land unto all the inhabitants thereof," a quote from Leviticus 25:10. From the statehouse tower, it was rung to announce important events, such as the coronation of King George III, the enactment of the Sugar Act in 1764, and the passage of the Stamp Act in 1765. On July 8, 1776, it proclaimed America's independence from Great Britain. The Liberty Bell cracked beyond repair in 1846 while being rung in celebration of George Washington's birthday. It was removed from its tower and placed on display on the ground floor of Independence Hall in 1852. On several occasions, including the Panama-Pacific Exposition in 1915 and bond rallies during World War I, the Liberty Bell was displayed in various locations across the country.

BETSY ROSS HOUSE PHILADELPHIA.

No visit to Philadelphia was complete without a trip to the Betsy Ross House at 239 Arch Street. The two-and-a-half-story, Georgian-style residence, known as "the birthplace of Old Glory," was built around 1740 and was the home of Elizabeth Griscom Ross Ashbourne Claypoole from 1773 until 1836. An upholsterer, seamstress, and flag maker by profession, Betsy Ross was purportedly asked by three members of the Continental Congress, George Washington, Robert Morris, and George Ross, to design and make a flag for the rebelling colonies in May 1776. Her flag, with alternating red and white stripes and 13 five-pointed stars on a blue field, was adopted by the Continental Congress on June 14, 1777, as the symbol of an emerging new nation, the United States of America. In 1892, more than two million patriotic Americans donated dimes to the Betsy Ross Memorial Association to restore the decaying property and convert the building to a national historic shrine.

Benjamin Franklin's grave, located in the Christ Church burial grounds at the corner of Fifth and Arch Streets, was one of the best-known landmarks in Philadelphia. Almost every visitor to the city made it a point to pay homage at the burial site of the man renowned as an author, scientist, inventor, statesman, and leading citizen. From his printing shop located at 532 High Street, Franklin had published *Poor Richard's Almanac*, complete with useful information and witty sayings, for more than 25 years. His famous electricity experiments in a thunderstorm with a kite and a key took place in the backyard of his home at Race and Second Streets. When Franklin died in 1790, more than 20,000 people took part in the funeral procession to Christ Church. The epitaph that Franklin wrote for himself at the age of 22 was carved upon marble tablets displayed at the site of the grave.

The U. S. Mint, Philadelphia, Pa.

Another destination for visitors, especially those with an interest in money, was the United States Mint. The Philadelphia Mint, the oldest in the country, was established in 1792 and was located on Seventh Street, above Market Street. This building, the second United States Mint, was located at Juniper and Chestnut Streets. Visitors could tour the coining operations and view the largest, most valuable collection of coins and metals in the nation.

The bear pits or dens at the Philadelphia Zoo were of interest to visitors not only because of their inhabitants but also because of their architectural significance. Among the earliest of the zoo's buildings, the bear pits were semicircular metal enclosures set into a knoll. Judging by the number of onlookers shown in this postcard, people were more interested in the bears that lived in the dens than they were in the history behind the cages.

Watching the Bears at the Zoo, Fairmount Park, Philadelphia, Pa.

2277

23

BABY ELEPHANT AND KEEPER ZOOLOGICAL GARDEN PHILADELPHIA

The baby elephant's quarters did not appear especially spacious in this postcard view, although the Elephant House had been designed by noted architects Furness and Hewitt. In reality, however, it was a huge structure with square towers and elevated stalls that allowed the animals to look down upon visitors walking through the building. Originally the zoo had just one elephant, named Jenny.

A postcard from the early 1900s showed female visitors in long pastel dresses and fashionable summer hats feeding the dromedary. Like the rhinoceros and other exotic animals, camels were a popular attraction at the zoo. Since they were rarely exhibited in circuses or traveling menageries, few visitors had ever seen them before.

No. 969. *Feeding the Dromedary Zoological Gardens, Philadelphia.*

TWO

# SOCIAL INSTITUTIONS

Underlying any great city are the social institutions—churches, museums, libraries, schools, and hospitals—that make society strong. Philadelphia possessed its share and more, benefiting both residents and visitors. A belief in the value of learning led to the development of numerous museums, libraries, schools, and institutions of higher education. Charitable organizations such as almshouses and hospitals were established. Founded on principles of religious freedom, the colony of Pennsylvania and its capital city attracted members of all religious denominations who built places in which to worship. William Penn and many of the other early residents of the city were members of the Society of Friends (Quakers), as were succeeding generations of leading Philadelphians. The Friends Arch Street Meeting House was built in 1804, taking the place of the Great Meeting House that dated from 1695 at Second and Market Streets. The Philadelphia Yearly Meeting of Friends, held each March, drew members from Pennsylvania, New Jersey, Delaware, and Maryland.

1635. FRIENDS MEETING HOUSE PHILADELPHIA, PA.

COPYRIGHT, 1905, BY DETROIT PUBLISHING CO.

Philadelphia—Christ Church.

Christ Church, built in 1727, was the third-oldest church building in Philadelphia. Located on the west side of Second Street, above Market Street, the building was begun in 1727 under the direction of Dr. John Kearsley. The installation of the famous chiming bells in the 200-foot tower and steeple marked its completion 27 years later. One of the largest churches in North America in the 18th century, Christ Church was a colonial adaptation of the Georgian architectural style of Christopher Wren's churches in London. Among the parishioners were many of the leaders of the American Revolution, including Robert Morris, John Dixon, Benjamin Franklin, Betsy Ross, and Charles Lee. As a group, the entire Continental Congress attended services at Christ Church in July 1775. Seven of the signers of the Declaration of Independence were buried on church grounds, while John Penn, the last male descendent of William Penn, was buried near the steps of the pulpit.

Dutch and Swedish fur traders were among the earliest inhabitants of what came to be called the Southwark section of Philadelphia. Gloria Dei, also known as Old Swedes Church, was built in the late 1600s on the site of an earlier Swedish log church near the Delaware River. It was the oldest church building in Pennsylvania and one of the oldest in continuous use in the United States.

A 3125a. Old Swedes Church, Philadelphia, Pa.

Cathedral of Sts. Peter and Paul,
18th and Race Streets,
Philadelphia, Pa.

Roman Catholics also found religious freedom in William Penn's colony. St. Mary's became the city's first Roman Catholic cathedral following the creation of Philadelphia as a separate diocese in 1808. In 1846, Bishop Francis P. Kenrick chose the site at Eighteenth and Race Streets for a new cathedral—SS. Peter and Paul. Designed by three architects and two priests, the cathedral was an outstanding example of Palladian Revival architecture and a focal point on Logan Square.

Priests at the new Cathedral of SS. Peter and Paul celebrated the first mass on Easter Sunday 1862, almost 16 years after construction began. The lavishly decorated cathedral contained the famous painting *Crucifixion* by Constantino Brumidi, the artist who also painted the dome in the nation's Capitol. Bishops and archbishops of the church were buried in the crypt.

MASONIC TEMPLE,
Philadelphia, Pa.

23625

Fraternal organizations held an important place in the City of Brotherly Love. The Masonic temple at Broad and Filbert Streets took five years to build because all of the stone had to be cut, squared, and marked at the quarries according to Masonic tradition. Completion of the elaborate interior required an additional 15 years. Worth the time and effort, the building held the distinction of being one of the world's most beautiful temples and was a definite Philadelphia landmark.

Although Benjamin Franklin was responsible for colonial mail service during his tenure as the first postmaster general, his working quarters were not nearly this elegant. Built on ground previously occupied by the University of Pennsylvania, the United States post office at Ninth, Chestnut, and Market Streets opened for business in 1884 after an 11-year period of construction and a cost of more than $7 million.

111 Post Office, Philadelphia, Pa.

Frankford Library.

44

Almost from its founding, Philadelphia had a wealth of libraries; all were either private or only open to members by subscription, however. Founded in 1891 with a $250,000 bequest by George Pepper, the Free Library was, as the name implied, the first of Philadelphia's libraries to be open to the general public free of charge. The Frankford Library was just one of 29 branch libraries operating under the auspices of Philadelphia's Free Library.

A $2 million bequest from the will of Stephen Girard led to the establishment of Girard College. A merchant, banker, and multimillionaire philanthropist, Girard was the wealthiest man in the United States at the time of his death in 1831. Opening on New Year's Day 1848, the school provided for the care and education of white male orphans between 6 and 18 years of age. Conditions for the admission gave preference to boys born in the following places: the old city of Philadelphia, the Commonwealth of Pennsylvania, New York City, and New Orleans. Founder's Hall, the central building of the campus and site of Girard's burial crypt, required 14 years to construct and was designed as the most impressive and archaeologically correct Greek temple in the United States.

507. PHILADELPHIA — GIRARD COLLEGE.

209. The Hahnemann College, Philadelphia, Pa.

Philadelphia had long been a center for medical education; the Medical Department of the University of Pennsylvania and Jefferson Medical College were two leading examples. A center to teach homeopathic medicine, the Homeopathic Medical College of Pennsylvania, was organized in 1848. Using a system of healing developed by Samuel Hahnemann, homeopathy treated diseases with small doses of drugs that were "capable of producing in healthy persons symptoms like those of the disease to be treated." A competing institution, Hahnemann Medical College, opened in 1867. The two homeopathic medical colleges merged in 1869 and combined with the Hospital of Philadelphia in 1885. Located at Broad and Race Streets, the oldest homeopathic medical college in the United States had 500 students and 700 patients.

What many considered it to be the foremost, unarguably the oldest of Philadelphia's institutions of higher education, was the University of Pennsylvania. In his pamphlet *Proposals Relating to the Education of Youth in Pennsylvania*, Benjamin Franklin advocated the establishment of a city academy and charitable school. Opened in 1751, the College, Academy, and Charitable School of Philadelphia officially became the University of Pennsylvania on September 30, 1791.

Thirty-Fourth Street Entrance to University of Pennsylvania
Philadelphia, Pa.

525-20

Drexel Institute, 33rd. and Chestnut Sts., Philadelphia, Pa.

The Drexel Institute of Art, Science, and Industry was founded in 1891 by Anthony J. Drexel. The wealthy financier wished to provide educational opportunities for young working-class men and women. Located at Thirty-second and Chestnut Streets, the school offered cooperative courses in engineering and business administration that allowed students to perform actual work in Philadelphia industries.

In 1836, legislation was passed guaranteeing the education of all children over the age of four. The state's first step toward compulsory education, it was also considered to be one of the greatest strides in free public instruction. By the end of 1925, Philadelphia boasted of having 277,859 pupils taught by 7,227 teachers in 371 school buildings, including the Northeast Manual Training School at Eighth Street and Lehigh Avenue.

· PHILADELPHIA ·
NORTHEAST MANUAL TRAINING SCHOOL.

Boys' Central High School,
Philadelphia, Pa.

The same legislation provided for the establishment of Central High School, the second-oldest high school in America. Alexander Dallas Bache, the great-grandson of Benjamin Franklin, served as the school's first principal in 1839. Originally located on Juniper Street, facing Center Square, the school later moved to Broad and Green Streets. Erected in 1900 at a cost of $1.5 million, this building was dedicated in 1902 by Pres. Theodore Roosevelt.

"Another one of our girls' schools," bragged the author of this postcard depicting the William Penn High School for Girls at Fifteenth and Wallace Streets. In 1925, the city had 11 senior high schools and 12 junior high schools, with a combined enrollment of 51,346 students. Construction was set to begin on the city's newest school, the Trade School for Girls.

Wm. Penn High School for Girls, 15th and Wallace Sts., Philadelphia, Pa.

THREE

# TRANSPORTATION, LODGING, AND ENTERTAINMENT

Visitors came to Philadelphia for many reasons during the first quarter of the 20th century. Some came for business, others for pleasure. Many recorded their visit through postcards. Sent to Michigan from Philadelphia in 1913, this postcard was one of a series that featured views of the city as seen from a balloon floating one mile above the landscape. Taken by William N. Jennings on the Fourth of July in 1893, the original photographs were the first aerial images of the city ever recorded. Fairmount Park and the Schuylkill River filled most of this postcard, giving the city a far less urban appearance than was really the case. In reality, Philadelphia had grown to be one of the world's largest cities by the beginning of the 20th century. Between 1890 and 1930, the number of residents more than doubled as waves of immigrants poured into the city. Philadelphia had also become a manufacturing and industrial giant.

Philadelphia, Pa. and Schuylkill River taken from Balloon 1 Mile high.

© W.N. JENNINGS

2347

Bird's-eye View of Schuylkill River, taken from Balloon 1 mile high, showing Regatta, Philadelphia, Pa.

©W.N.JENNINGS

2346

Another image in the Jennings balloon series of photographs showed a view of the Schuylkill River with a regatta in progress. While this postcard also led viewers to assume that Philadelphia was a small town nestled in a pastoral setting, the reality was much different. Other views in the aerial series presented views of a densely populated metropolitan area.

From the tower of Independence Hall looking to the west along Chestnut Street, the city unfolded. The closest buildings were the oldest, many dating from the colonial period. Beyond them were newer commercial buildings and a few modern skyscrapers. City hall (background, far right) was the tallest building in the city at the time of this photograph. This remained true for many years to come.

Bird's Eye View from Independence Hall, Philadelphia, Pa.

Down at street level, pedestrians had a similar view of the city. Known as "juggernauts of death," the first electric streetcars had been introduced in 1892. As the automobile increased in popularity, horse-drawn vehicles, automobiles, and electric trolley cars competed for space on the city's narrow streets, resulting in massive traffic congestion. It was frequently quicker to walk to nearby destinations.

Philadelphia was famous for the layout of its streets, the plan for which was designed by William Penn. While the original city covered just two square miles, by 1925 there were more than 1,718 miles of streets. In 1684, Penn ordered the cross streets to be named numerically, while the east-west streets were to be named after local trees: Cedar, Pine, Spruce, Chestnut, Mulberry, Sassafras, and Vine.

5251 Chestnut Street, looking west, Philadelphia, Pa.

Running east and west from the Delaware River to Sixty-ninth Street, Market Street was the dividing line between the north and south sides of the city. It was also the center of the retail district in center-city Philadelphia. Many of the large department stores for which the city was famous, including John Wanamaker, Gimbel Brothers, Strawbridge and Clothier, Lit Brothers, and Snellenburg's, were located along Market Street.

William Penn's original design for Philadelphia called for a gridiron pattern of wide streets that intersected large public squares. While most of the streets had a width of only 50 feet, his plan called for High (now known as Market) and Broad Streets to be 100 feet wide, exceeding the widest streets in 17th-century London. Broad Street, 12 miles long, was claimed, albeit erroneously, to be the world's longest street.

Dock St. Market below Walnut, Philadelphia, Pa.

2333

One of the city's earliest commercial areas, Dock Street, ran southeast from Second and Walnut Streets to the Delaware River. While the original Dock Street Market area was much smaller, this center for Philadelphia's fruit and produce supply had expanded to fill all of Dock Street as well as many of the surrounding side streets. While the stores and stalls were always busy, the streets were filled with vehicles of every description on market days.

Rittenhouse Square was one of the four smaller squares set aside as public parks in William Penn's design. Situated between Eighteenth Street on the east, Nineteenth Street on the west, and Walnut Street on the north, it was one of Philadelphia's most elegant and fashionable neighborhoods. Surrounded by the homes of the city's wealthiest citizens, the square itself provided a playground for their children.

Philadelphia, Pa. Rittenhouse Square and Holy Trinity Church.

Philadelphia was served by three major railroads—the Pennsylvania, the Reading, and the Baltimore and Ohio. Located adjacent to city hall at Twelfth and Market Streets was the pink brick Renaissance-style Reading Terminal. Completed in 1893, the terminal's train shed was the world's oldest long-span roof structure.

OPPOSITE: The train shed for the Pennsylvania Railroad's Broad Street Station was considered to be a technological wonder. Engineered by Wilson Brothers and Company in 1893, the arched-glass shed had the world's largest permanent roof, with a span of 300 feet, eight inches. A catastrophic fire destroyed it in 1923.

Broad St. Station from Switch Tower, Philadelphia, Pa.

Whether aboard the Market Street Ferry operated by the Pennsylvania Railroad or the Chestnut Street Ferry run by the Philadelphia and Reading Railroad, ferry transportation provided a quick and inexpensive way for those without private transportation to reach Camden, New Jersey. This enabled many to partake of a popular summer pastime—a visit to the seaside towns of the New Jersey shore.

Ferry Boat crossing the Delaware, Philadelphia, Pa.

For visitors and residents alike, there were several ways to get around the city. For those without a horse-drawn vehicle or one of the increasingly popular automobiles, a number of types of public transportation existed. Formed in 1902, the Philadelphia Rapid Transit Company ran the electric-powered trolley system. To relieve traffic congestion, the company began to build an elevated railroad system along Market Street in 1903.

During the same period, construction of a connecting underground subway system was undertaken. When the task of building and maintaining both elevated and underground lines became too much for a private company, the city agreed to build the lines and lease them to the Philadelphia Rapid Transit Company. The Market Street subway was the first to be constructed.

The major department stores were quick to realize the potential benefits of the subway. Customers were rapidly delivered to the downtown shopping area, avoiding the headaches of growing traffic congestion. Basement entrances from the subway stations allowed shoppers to be lured into the big stores without being exposed to competition from other shops along the street.

Philadelphia's largest and most splendid hotel—the Bellevue-Stratford at the corner of Broad and Walnut Streets—was described as "representative of the increasing lust for uninhibited opulence which marked virtually all of the great hostelries of the period." George Boldt, the son of a German immigrant, created the 19-story, 937-room hotel as part of an effort to attract out-of-town visitors. Opening in 1902, the hotel unabashedly touted its amenities, including Turkish and Swedish baths, a library, two in-house orchestras, three ballrooms, and an outdoor rose garden on the roof. Some 15,000 pieces of furniture in a variety of styles decorated rooms that were cleaned by 100 chambermaids and 59 cleaners using pneumatic sweeping. Each room also contained a safe for protection of a guest's valuable possessions.

With three ballrooms and numerous other areas suitable for entertaining, the Bellevue-Stratford quickly became a part of the social scene. As the society news sections of local newspapers reported the comings and goings of fashionable Philadelphians, the Bellevue-Stratford was the hotel most frequently mentioned.

For John Wanamaker, bigger meant better. On February 22, 1902, ground was broken for a new store—one that Wanamaker himself modestly termed "the largest and most beautiful building in the world devoted to retail merchandising." The new structure was completed almost 10 years later, just in time for the store's 50th anniversary celebration. The 12-story granite building had nearly two million square feet of floor area, 50 passenger elevators, 19 freight elevators, and its own power and refrigeration plants. Telephones for public use were located near every counter to be used free of charge for calls from one part of the store to another. A post office, cable and telegraph center, stenographic service, and visitors' headquarters provided additional amenities. Wanamaker Field, located on the roof, offered a running track, plus basketball and tennis courts. The new store was truly a "palace of commerce."

John Wanamaker's New Store, from City Hall Place, Philadelphia, Pa.

Eight St. looking north from Filbert St., Philadelphia, Pa.

Although each neighborhood had its share of small shops, by the beginning of the 20th century, the major retail district of Philadelphia was centered along Chestnut and Market Streets, between Fifth and Broad Streets. Along these streets were the large department stores for which Philadelphia was famous. This postcard shows that Eighth Street at Filbert Street was the prime shopping area for shoes.

To attract customers, Lit Brothers Department Store used a number of marketing tricks—hats trimmed free of charge, double yellow trading stamps with every purchase before noon, and a Victor phonograph record club with a $1 monthly membership fee. A customer in 1907 wrote to a friend in New York, "This is the store we are going to. They don't close until 10 but it will take us that long to go through. There is so much to see."

Strawbridge and Clothier's,
8th and Market Streets,
Philadelphia, Pa.

Strawbridge and Clothier called itself "Philadelphia's Foremost Store." Although this may have appeared to be a rather unseemly boast for a company founded and patronized by Quakers, in the minds of many Philadelphians, it was a true statement. The store was also one of the first to provide certain amenities, including lunchrooms and building and loan associations, for its workers.

Looking like the quintessential Victorian ice-cream parlor, Childs' Place was a popular eating spot. Another restaurant of the same name was located in the New Jersey seaside resort of Atlantic City. On this postcard, mailed to New York City in 1907, Irving inquired, "Can you guess where I had lunch?"

11569—A Good Place in Philadelphia, Pa.

Philadelphia Opera House and Broad Street, Philadelphia, Pa.

214511

104

Famed theatrical impresario Oscar Hammerstein opened the Philadelphia Opera House at Broad and Poplar Streets in 1908 with a performance of Bizet's *Carmen*. Wealthy and socially prominent Philadelphians filled the horseshoe boxes and dress circle seats for performances by the leading opera stars of the day. Four operatic performances each week during the performance season were not enough, however, to make the lavishly appointed theater successful. Facing a $400,000 mortgage, Hammerstein relinquished the venture to E. T. Stotesbury, who renamed it the Metropolitan Opera House. With the largest stage in the city, the opera house seated 3,791 music lovers. Competition from the Academy of Music eventually led to the demise of the opera house, reducing it to the status of a motion picture theater. In 1920, it was leased to the members of Lulu Temple, a fraternal organization.

Providing good food at inexpensive prices, the Horn and Hardart Baking Company's Automats quickly gained popularity with visitors and residents alike. The Automat at 818–820 Chestnut Street claimed to be the world's largest automatic restaurant.

OPPOSITE: One Automat advertisement appealed to busy workers trying to squeeze in a few errands on their lunch hour. "Miss Quick" was shown arriving at the Automat at noon. She made her selection of chicken croquette with green peas, a roll, hot chocolate, and apple cake for dessert—all for just 40¢. Finished eating by 12:20, she was now free to enjoy the remainder of her lunch hour to shop or stroll.

EAST RIVER DRIVE AT RIDGE AVENUE, FAIRMOUNT PARK, PHILADELPHIA, PA.

2253

The East River Drive was considered unsurpassed for its scenic beauty in the early 1920s. Winding through Fairmount Park along the Schuylkill River, the street ran past the city aquarium in the old waterworks; Mount Pleasant, Benedict Arnold's former residence; the Lincoln monument; and Grant's log cabin. It was also an excellent vantage point from which to view the races on the river in front of Boathouse Row.

As the first quarter of the 20th century ended, a monumental event kicked off the next 25 years. The Philadelphia sesquicentennial, which began on May 31, 1926, was intended to draw 50 million visitors to celebrate the 150th birthday of the United States. Fourth of July activities included a speech by Pres. Calvin Coolidge, as well as a historical pageant with over 2,500 participants. A cyclone coaster offered breakneck thrills at speeds over 100 miles an hour.

52:—MAIN ENTRANCE, BROAD STREET,

SESQUI-CENTENNIAL INTERNATIONAL EXPOSITION, PHILADELPHIA, PA.

FOUR

# BUSINESS

Philadelphia's growth as a center of commerce was apparent in the development of large commercial skyscrapers, such as the Betz Building, the Girard, and the Real Estate Trust. Despite the business constraints imposed by World War I, the Real Estate Trust Company advertised "$1,000,000 of capital (full paid) and $1,800,000 surplus and undivided profits" on January 12, 1918.

The skyscraping North American Building on Sansom Street was home to the oldest daily newspaper in America. Founded in 1784, the newspaper was an outgrowth of Benjamin Franklin's *Pennsylvania Gazette*. Long a leader in the fight for political reform, the *North American* merged with the *Public Ledger* on May 18, 1925.

Purchased in 1889 by James Elverson, the *Philadelphia Inquirer* became one of the most successful morning newspapers in the nation. By 1914, it was the third-largest newspaper in the United States in terms of advertising sales. In 1924, the *Inquirer* moved into its new headquarters in the Elverson Building, an Italian Renaissance–style edifice of white limestone and terra cotta. The tall commercial building's clock tower was topped with a dome and lantern, making it especially visible at night.

114 ELVERSON BUILDING AT NIGHT.

HOME OF THE PHILA. INQUIRER, PHILADELPHIA, PA.

The Curtis Publishing Company, Independence Square, Philadelphia, Pa.
The Ladies Home Journal—The Saturday Evening Post—The Country Gentleman.

2592

Home to the publishing houses of Lippencott's and Carey & Lea, Philadelphia had a long-standing reputation as a literary center. In 1883, a newcomer entered the publishing arena and soon came to dominate the market. Constructed in the 1890s, the Georgian-style building housing the Curtis Publishing Company was situated at 601–645 Walnut Street and occupied an entire city block. Headquarters for three leading magazines of the era, *Ladies Home Journal*, *Country Gentleman*, and the *Saturday Evening Post*, the multistoried red brick building towered over neighboring historic structures such as Independence Hall and Carpenters' Hall. By 1916, the Curtis Publishing Company had become one of the city's largest white-collar businesses, employing more than 3,000 Philadelphians that year.

Covers of the *Saturday Evening Post* featured the work of some of the nation's best-known artists and illustrators. N. C. Wyeth, J. C. Leyendecker, Harrison Fischer, John Falter, Steven Dohanos, and Norman Rockwell were all contributors to the magazine. The magazine's artwork soon became as much a reason for purchase as its content.

Section of Engraving Department
*The Curtis Publishing Company, Philadelphia*

The Ladies' Home Journal
The Saturday Evening Post
The Country Gentleman

220. League Island Navy Yard, Philadelphia, Pa.

By 1925, the League Island Navy Yard, at the south end of Broad Street, was the largest navy yard in the world, occupying 923 acres. A full regiment of marines and as many as 7,000 sailors were usually stationed there. The yard employed more than 25,000 people during the final months of World War I. When reopened for public tours, more than 100,000 people visited the facility in a single day.

Philadelphia had a long-standing maritime tradition. Cramp's Shipyard occupied a large section of the Delaware River front above Market Street. The William Cramp and Sons Ship and Engine Building Company had been home to naval and merchant marine construction and shipping since its founding in 1830. In its yard, *New Ironsides*, the first ironclad craft of the U.S. Navy, was constructed in only 11 months.

2366—Cramp's Shipyard, Philadelphia, Pa.

Hello Dewitt:- How are you getting along
weather since I am working in Clayville. Mrs. Gibson
Clayville

Arcadia Publishing is the leading local history publisher in the United States. With more than 3,000 titles in print and hundreds of new titles released every year, Arcadia has extensive specialized experience chronicling the history of communities and celebrating America's hidden stories, bringing to life people, places, and events from the past. To discover the history of other communities across the nation, please visit:

## www.arcadiapublishing.com

Customized search tools allow you to find regional history books about the town where you grew up, the cities where your friends and relatives live, the town where your parents met, or even that retirement spot you've been dreaming of. The Arcadia website also provides history lovers with exclusive deals, advanced notice of new titles, e-mail alerts of author events, and much more.